JEWISH HOLIDAY FUN

DAVID A. ADLER

WORD FINDS

POEMS

PUZZLES

MAZES

SCRAMBLES

JOKES

REBUSES

RIDDLES...and MORE!

KAR-BEN COPIES INC.   ROCKVILLE, MD

ISBN 0930494-72-5
Published by KAR-BEN COPIES, INC. Rockville, MD
Printed in the United States of America

Cover by Roz Schanzer

CONTENTS

DON'T READ THE BOOK

Don't read the book
about the bent Lulav.
There's no point to it.

Don't read the book
about the Shabbat dinner.
It's fowl.

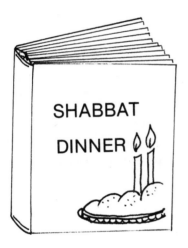

Don't read the book
about the broken matzah.
It's crummy.

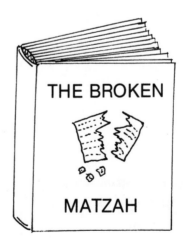

Don't read the book
about the schach (the roof
of a sukkah).
It's over your head.

Don't read the book
about the 288 hamantaschen.
It's two gross.

But you should read the book
about bread on Passover.
It's outa' sight.

And you should read the book
about the New Year.
It's sweet.

A SHABBAT MAZE

It's Shabbat. You live in the house at the top of the maze and you want to walk to visit your friends. Can you find a path to each of the other houses in the maze?

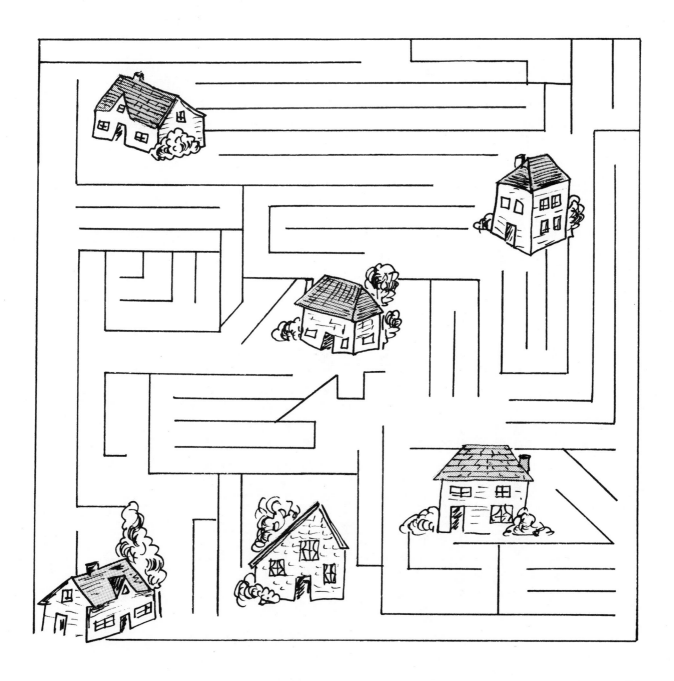

Answer on page 59.

HOLIDAY SEARCH

Can you find the following holidays in the letters below? Circle the holidays as you find them.

Shabbat
Rosh Hashanah
Yom Kippur
Sukkot
Rosh Chodesh

Hoshana Rabba
Shemini Azeret
Simchat Torah
Chanukah

Tu B'Shevat
Purim
Passover
Yom Hashoah

Yom Ha'Azmaut
Lag B'Omer
Yom Yerushalayim
Shavuot
Tishah B'Av

```
S H A B B A T H A P P Y H O L I D A Y S D P R E
N U S A Q R E T Y R O S H L U L A V Z I U A H F
E T R O G H F D C H O D E S H S H O F A R S O Y
M E N O R A H H A D A S S I M S E D E R M S W E
T R E E H R O S H M H A S H A N A H O N E O N E
S W R O A M A T Z A H A R A V O T N I N E V E R
I T P Y S M N T U I B S H E V A T U Y T E E B Z
M O I O H K A R B E N C O P I E S G H R T R O P
C R T M O L U L A T I S H A H U I S H E M I N I
H A Y R A N B V R E B A V B M O I A Z E R E T L
A H K I H J E W I S H H O L I D A Y F U N M B Y
T M S H A V U O T Z I M S U K K O T M A T Z A H
K A R B E N C O P I E S B O O K H E T R O G B I
C H A N U K A H Y O M C P U Y T A M L A G H A T
Y O M B V U I Y T E R W U O N E A B O M E R L J
Y E R U S H A L A Y I M R O T Y Z H A P P Y W E
C H I L D R E N W A L D I Y T O M N O A M A R I
Y O M H K I P P U R B R M B A M A P O U Y T R E
R E A D H E A V E N H A P P Y N U N B V C E S W
F O U R H O S H A N A C O U N T T M B E W Y O U
B C E S E R A B B A M I C H A E L R E D W A R D
```

Two-word holidays may be separated. Be careful!

Answer on page 59.

8

HOLIDAY REBUS

In each box is the rebus of another holiday. Do you know what they are?

1. _____

2. _____

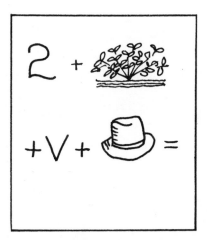

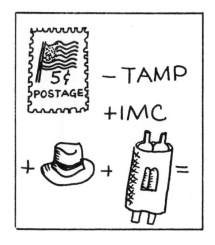

3. _____

4. _____

Answers on page 59.

9

A SCRAMBLED SHABBAT

Below are four words relating to Shabbat, the day of rest. But the letters are scrambled. Can you unscramble them?

1. _____

2. _____

3. _____

4. _____

Answers on page 59.

CANDLESTICK PUZZLE

Can you tell which of the six pieces below is the missing piece in this drawing of two Shabbat candlesticks?

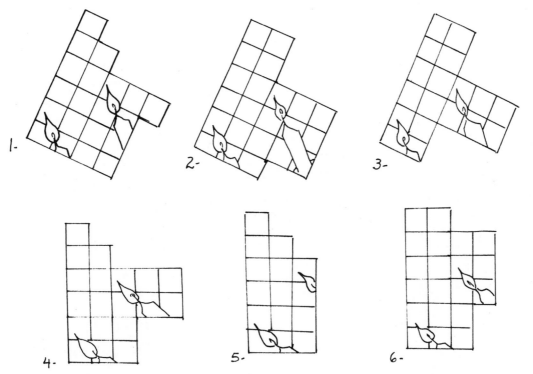

1-

2-

3-

4-

5-

6-

Answer on page 59.

CHALLAH RIDDLES

What's brown, yellow and jumpy?

A challah covered with hoppy seeds.

Why would anyone baking a challah mix shoe polish with the yeast?

So the challah would rise and shine.

Which is the left side of a challah?

The side you haven't eaten.

What's the best thing you could put into a challah?

Your teeth.

Which of our fifty states is filled with white bread and bathing suits?

Challahfornia.

HOLIDAY PICTURE RIDDLES

Below are five picture riddles. Can you tell what they are?

1. _____

2. _____

PASS

3. _____

4. _____

MY TEACHERS, PARENTS, AND FRIENDS ALL PICK ON ME. IT'S ALWAYS, "HERB DO THIS, HERB DO THAT..."

5. _____

Answers on page 59.

SWEET, SWEET SAM

Sweet,
sweet,
sweet
brother Sam.
He's much better
than you or I am.
He's so good
and he's so sweet.
He's got honeycombs
instead of feet.
He's got gumdrops
instead of eyes.
And his ears
are apple pies.
And on the New Year
we dip apple in honey.
And we dip some in Sam.
Now isn't that funny!

Can you draw Sweet Sam?

AN APPLE AND HONEY MAZE

On Rosh Hashanah, the Jewish New Year, we eat apple dipped in honey and pray for a sweet New Year. See if you can find a path through the apples and honey to the sweet New Year at the bottom of the maze. Then count the number of apples and jars of honey in the maze.

SWEET NEW YEAR

Answer on page 59.

A HOLIDAY MEMORY QUIZ

Look at the ten holiday items on the page. Then close the book and see how many of them you can remember.

THE MISSING PIECE

A shofar, ram's horn, is blown on Rosh Hashanah as a call to repentance. A piece of the shofar drawing below is missing. Can you find the missing piece?

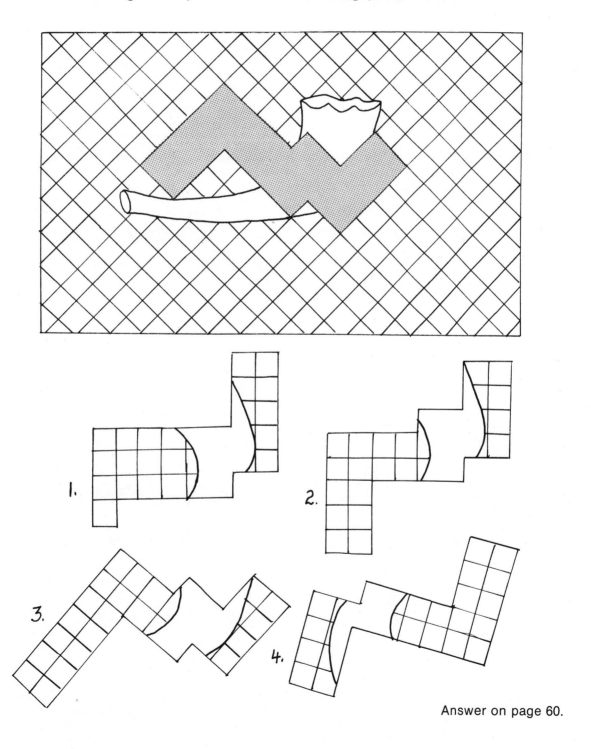

Answer on page 60.

A SCRAMBLED NEW YEAR

Below are four words relating to Rosh Hashanah, the Jewish New Year. But the letters are scrambled. Can you unscramble them?

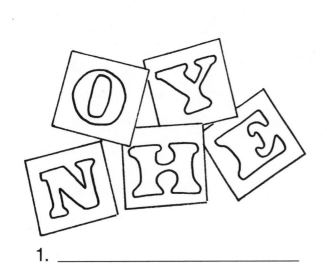

1. _____

2. _____

3. _____

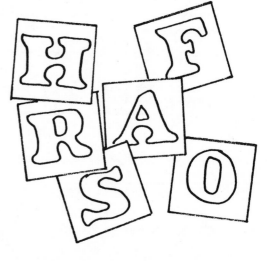

4. _____

Answers on page 60.

YOM KIPPUR HIDDEN DRAWING

Shade in only the shapes with one of the letters in YOM KIPPUR and a hidden drawing will appear.

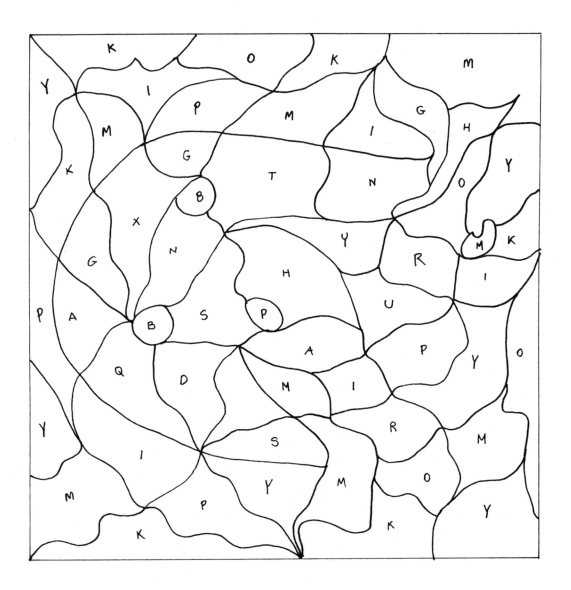

AN ETROG NAMED SUE

I had an etrog.
I called it Sue.
I taught that etrog
everything I knew.
Then one day
Sue put on a gown,
hopped on a bus
and rode out of town.

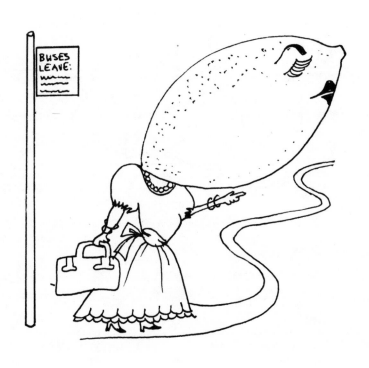

SUKKOT MAZE

Without crossing any lines, find your way to your own Sukkah. It's the one with the open door at the bottom of the maze.

START HERE

Answer on page 60.

JEWISH HOLIDAY BUMMERS

Chanukah latkes that are hot, brown, and oily on the outside and still frozen inside.

Shabbat candles without wicks.

Chanukah gifts you can wear.

Homework over vacation.

When your aunt pinches your cheek and says you're cute.

When your mother makes you give Chanukah gelt (money) back to your uncle because it's too much.

Prune hamantaschen.

When you put on a Purim costume and everyone knows it's you.

A dreidel which keeps landing on ש.

THE SUKKAH CHAIN

Many people decorate their sukkah with fruits and colorful chains. Below is a sukkah chain. But not all the links are connected. Can you find the ten links which are not connected to the main chain?

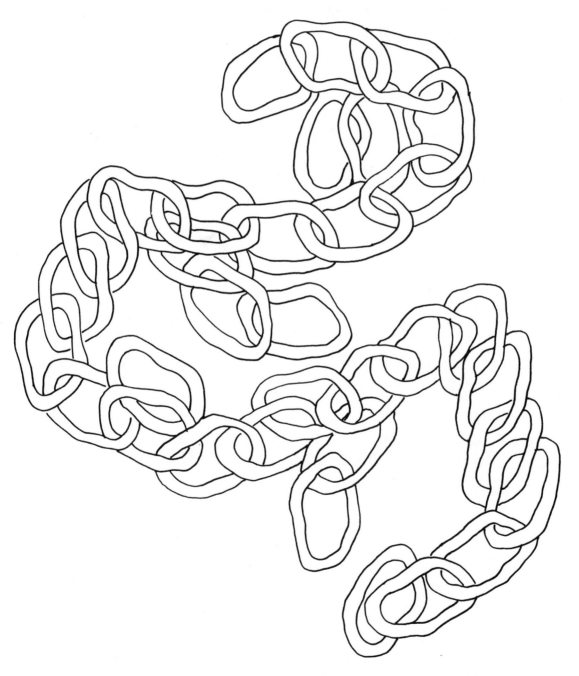

Answer on page 60.

HIDDEN HOLIDAY MESSAGES

1. Take out every F, G, J and V.

   GFTHEF GSJHVAJVBBATF
   FJCGAVNDJLEF GTGOLD FTHEFV
   GJMAGTVCHG FYOUF GBFUVRN MEJ GUPF.

2. Take out every B, D, E and F.

   EMEATZDABHF FISE BDEFCREFUMEDMBY.

3. Take out every B, C, G and H.

   FBACSGTH BDACYS HARGEH GSGLGOGW
   CDBAHYGS.

4. Take out every C, D, N and R.

   DIN CDGNIRVER DMNRYC DLUDLDARVC
   DTCHER CSNHADKERS.

5. Take out every C, G, L and U.

   GSGHLAUBUBALT LIGSU UNELVELUR
   UMLOREG THALNUG SLIXUL GLDALGYUS
   GALWLAUYLUG.

Answers on page 60.

LULAV, ETROG, ARAVOT and HADASSIM

During Sukkot we hold together and shake 1 lulav (palm branch), 1 etrog (citron), 2 aravot (willow branches), and 3 hadassim (myrtle bush branches). It has been said that the lulav, etrog, aravot and hadassim which are each different from the other, represent the Jewish people who are also all different but who should all work together.

See how many lulav sets you can find below.

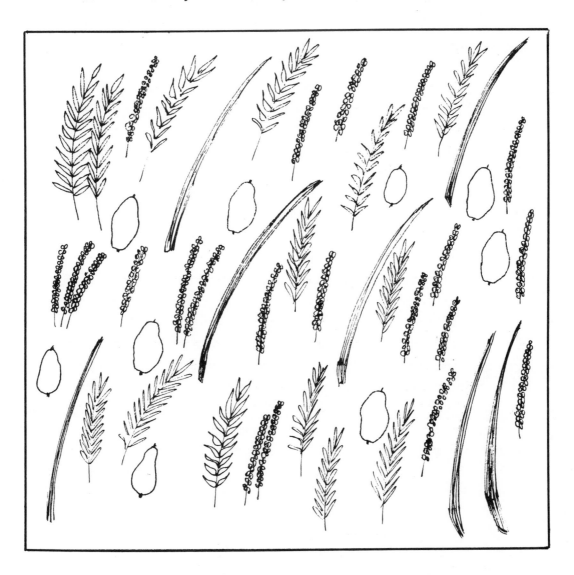

Answer on page 60.

SHEMINI AZERET

Shemini Azeret is celebrated right after the holiday of Sukkot.

How many different words can you make using the letters in SHEMINI AZERET?

More than 80 of the many possible answers are given on page 60.

_____   _____
_____   _____
_____   _____
_____   _____
_____   _____
_____   _____
_____   _____
_____   _____
_____   _____
_____   _____
_____   _____
_____   _____
_____   _____
_____   _____
_____   _____
_____   _____
_____   _____
_____   _____
_____   _____
_____   _____
_____   _____
_____   _____

Thermofax

SIMCHAT TORAH REBUS

Some of the words and sounds in the story below have been replaced with pictures. See if you can read the story.

On Simchat [Torah scroll], the day the reading of the **5** [books] of Moses was completed & [bee][hand pointing] again, th[eye] was gr[8] joy. Rabbis who studied the [Torah scroll] all y[eye] were singing & d[ant][worm]ing & so were th[eye] students. But the [1] who was celebr[8]ting the most was a poor [tailor].

"YRU so haP?" some[1] asked the [tailor]. "U did [knot] stu[D] the [Torah] all y[eye]. U did [knot] even lis[10] w[bird] it was [bee]ing read on Shabbat & holidays."

"[eye] don't stu[D] the [Torah] [bee]cause [eye] [can]'t," the [tailor] [ant][ant]ered. "[eye] [can]'t read Hebrew & [eye] don't understand it. But [eye] [can] d[ant][ant] & sing as [well] as NE1, so t[hat] is what [eye] do."

Answer on page 60.

27

CHANUKAH PUZZLES

Who lost the game of dreidel?

Sara's daughter Jane played dreidel until Jane called out, "I won!"

"I don't mind losing," the other player said, "since it's my daughter who won."

If Sara didn't lose, who did?

One dollar is missing

Three brothers bought three menorahs for a total of $60. After the brothers left the store, the shopkeeper realized he had made a mistake. The menorahs should have been sold for $55. He gave his clerk $5 and told him to run after the brothers. Each brother took one dollar from the clerk. The brothers thanked him, wished him a happy Chanukah and told him to keep the extra $2.

With the $1 the clerk returned to each brother, they paid a total of $57 for the menorahs. Add to the $57 the $2 the clerk kept and you have just $59. What happened to the other dollar?

Boxed

How would you put 7 candles into 4 boxes so that there's an odd number of candles in each box?

Answers on page 61.

CANDLE PUZZLES

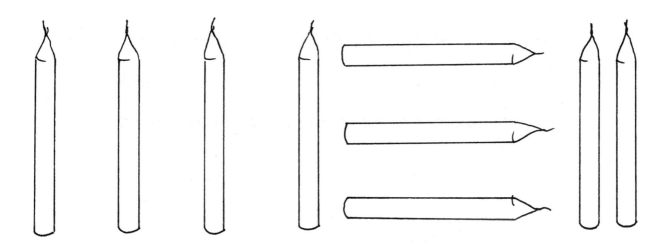

Arrange nine Chanukah candles as shown above. Then move two candles, add two candles, and be left with one.

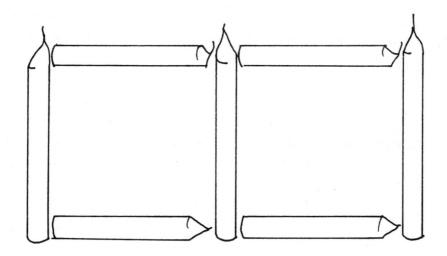

Arrange seven Chanukah candles to form two squares as shown above. Then add just five more candles to make three more squares.

Answers on page 61.

CHANUKAH RIDDLES

What time is it when you sit on a burning candle?

Springtime.

How can you light a Chanukah candle without a match?

Take a candle out of the box and the box will become a candle lighter.

Why did the foolish cook run out of the house when he was making latkes?

Because the recipe said, "Take one egg and beat it."

What has four sides, spins and hops?

A dreidel with hiccups.

Why won't the old candlemaker make candles any longer?

Because the candles are long enough.

If a candle and a half need a wick and a half, how long would it take a candlemaker to make a candle using noodles and soup?

Give up? So did the candlemaker.

DREIDEL MAZE

In the game of dreidel, each player puts a coin, raisin, or candy in the center. Then players take turns spinning the dreidel. If the dreidel lands with the נ facing up, the player does nothing. If the ג is facing up, the player wins the whole pot. If the ה is facing up, the player wins half the pot. If the ש is facing up, the player must put an extra coin, raisin, or candy in the center.

Try to find a path through this dreidel maze to the ג without first coming to one of the other letters.

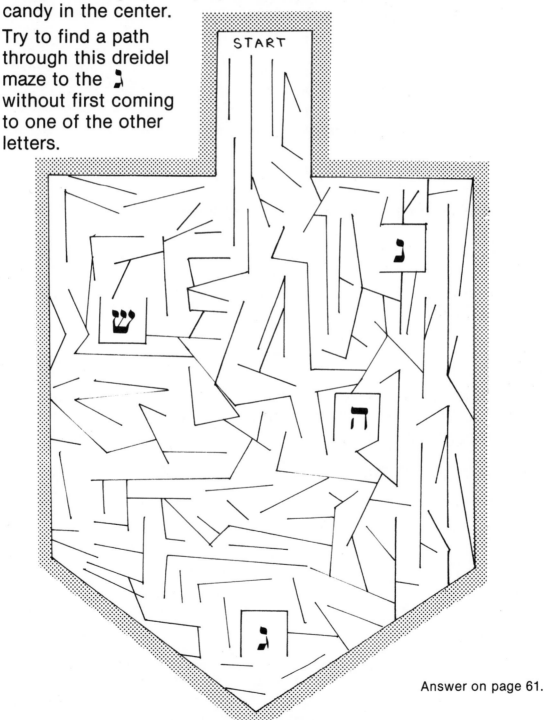

Answer on page 61.

HOLIDAY CROSSWORD PUZZLE

ACROSS

1. Chanukah lights.
6. Gold or silver.
7. Ten commandments were on _____ tablets.
9. The holiday of Esther and Mordecai.
11. Tu B'Shevat is the New Year for _____.
12. The opposite of yes.
13. Passover song: "Who _____ One?
15. Purim villain.
18. Israeli fruit.
20. The eleventh Hebrew month.
21. Citron.
23. Hebrew month of Shavuot.
24. Companion of 21 across.

DOWN

1. Wine mug.
2. Rhymes with "4."
3. What we do with four cups of wine on Passover.
4. Israeli fruit.
5. Opposite of found.
7. _____ Commandments.
8. You and I.
10. Opposite of over.
11. The fast day in Av.
14. Passover song: "Who Knows _____?"
16. Same as 20 across.
17. The Hebrew month for Passover.
19. The English month for Passover.
22. Chanukah fuel for lights.

Answer on page 61.

DANGLED WICKS

The wicks of these Chanukah candles have become tangled. Can you find the one which belongs to the shaded candle.

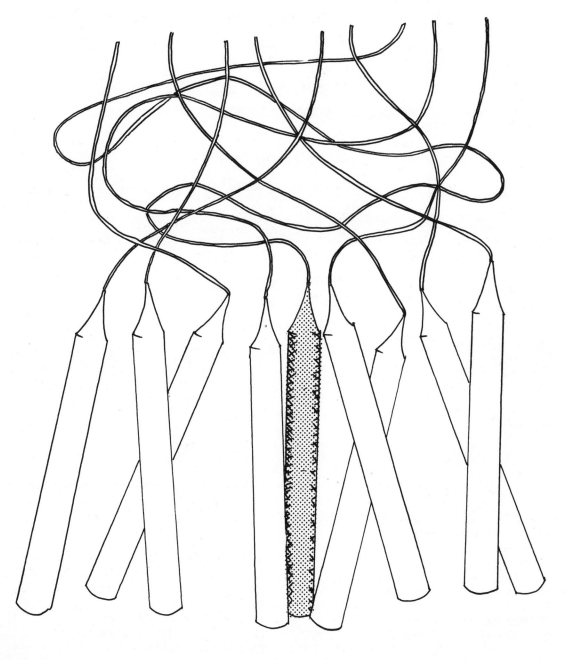

Answer on page 61.

I LIKE LATKES

I like latkes.
They taste fine.
I'll put potatoes
and oil in mine.
I'll put in butter
and lots of salt,
strawberry jam
and chocolate malt.
Vinegar, bubble gum,
peanuts and paste,
carrot juice, jelly
and lemon to taste.
I like latkes.
They taste fine.
But I'd never, ever
eat one of mine.

CHANUKAH HIDDEN DRAWING

Shade in only the shapes with one of the letters in
CHANUKAH and a hidden drawing will appear.

SCRAMBLED HOLIDAYS

Below are the names of three Jewish holidays. But the letters are scrambled. Can you unscramble them?

1. _____   2. _____

3. _____

Answers on page 62.

A TU B'SHEVAT MAZE

Tu B'Shevat is the New Year for trees. We celebrate by eating fruits and nuts. See if you can find a path through the maze of branches and leaves to the fruits below— without crossing any lines.

Answer on page 62.

SURE BETS

Just before Rosh Hashanah, give a friend a pencil and a sheet of paper. Then tell your friend, "Write a New Year's message on the paper, cover the paper with your hand, and I'll bet I can tell you what is on the paper."

After your friend writes the message and covers it, tell him what's on the paper. "Your hand."

On Chanukah hold up a dreidel and tell a friend, "Whenever you spin a dreidel it always stops. I'll bet I can make this dreidel never stop spinning."

Then just don't spin the dreidel. If it isn't spinning, how can it *stop* spinning!

On Passover tell your friend, "I'll bet I can put a matzah down in the middle of the room and you won't be able to jump over it."

Then, when your friend takes the bet, put the matzah on his head.

PICK SOME FRUIT

Tu B'Shevat is the new year for trees. It is celebrated on the fifteenth day of the Hebrew month of Shevat which falls in January or February.

Trees are very important in Israel. They keep soil from washing away, and they provide shade and fruit. In Israel on Tu B'Shevat, seedlings are planted. Here on the holiday, many people eat fruit grown in Israel. See if you can "pick the fruit" off this tree. Each time you find the word "fruit" circle it. There are 25 "fruits" on this tree.

```
                        H O F
                      C G U T R
                      T R E E U
                  F R U I T N O I B I G
                  N U T F R U I T T R E E
                F R U I T G T U M B I S H E V
                Y O U R F M O F V E T I U R F
              C D R E W P O R M O R T R E E S R
              F R U I T O F R U I T U T R E E U
          T U B I S H E V A T I M N I H O Y I
          F R U I T B V E U I T T O P T E W T
          M N B Y U T R F R U I T I S R A E L N
          U I Y K I T I U R F B V F R U I T L O F
          B F R U I T I S R A E L B R F R U I T R
      N I N E F R U I T I N F R U I T F O U R U
      T R E E S     F R U I T T I U R F S A I
      F R U I T     T R E E S         C A T
                    F R U I T
                    R O T T
                    U J R I
                    I O U U
                    T H N R
                    D E K F
                  R O O T S
                  G F E W A U
```

Hint: A few "fruits" appear backwards and two appear diagonally.

Answer on page 62.

MORE HOLIDAY BUMMERS

When you wear a monster disguise on Purim, and everyone tells you that you look better.

When your parents tell everyone that you're too old to get Chanukah presents.

When your younger brother tells everyone where you hid the afikomen.

When the last game of the World Series is on Yom Kippur.

When it rains on your Lag B'Omer picnic.

When you are making hamantaschen, and you forget what you already put in the bowl.

When your "big" part in the Chanukah play is to be the fifth candle.

When you ask for a pet in exchange for the afikomen, and your parents give you a stuffed animal.

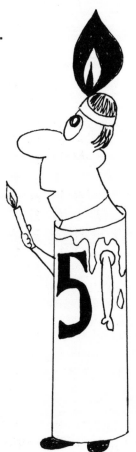

PURIM REBUS

On Purim, Megillat Esther, the Scroll of Esther, is read. Here's a shortened form of the story. Some of the words have been replaced with pictures. See if you can read it.

Ahasuerus was [king] of the Persian M[pie]re. He gave a **7** day feast. Vash[tea], the [queen], gave a feast **4** the women. On the **7**th day, Ahasuerus called **4** Vash[tea] **2** come [bee]**4** him. Vash[tea] refused **2** come **&** was ¢ away.

The [king]'s [men] searched **4** some**1** **2** repl[♥] Vash[tea]. They found a Jewish [girl], **S**ter. She [bee]came the new [queen].

Ster's cousin Mordecai lived in the [cap]ital of [shoe]shan. He re[fuse]sed **2** bow **2** the [king]'s chief minister, Haman. Haman t[hen] planned **2** kill all the Jews. Ahasuerus [told] him he could.

Mordecai [told] **S**ter w[hat] was about **2** ha[pen] **2** her P[people]. She spoke **2** the [king] **&** the Jews were saved.

Answer on page 62.

HAMAN CAME IN

What's a *Haman Came In?* It's a Jewish Holiday riddle which has a rhyming answer.

For example: What would you call someone who passes the appetizers at the Shabbat dinner table? A *Chopped Liver Giver,* of course!

Now try these:

1. What would you call a Purim snack?

   _____

2. What do you eat and eat and eat on Passover?

   _____

3. What would you call a large spoon used to serve Chanukah tops?

   _____

4. What would you call the Purim queen's teacher?

   _____

5. What dance is done on Simchat Torah?

   _____

6. What would you use to carry a box of Chanukah lights?

   _____

7. What would you call a Scroll of Esther written on heavy brown paper?

   _____

Answers on page 62.

HOW MANY HAMANTASCHEN?

On Purim we eat hamantaschen, triangular-shaped cakes filled with either a mixture of poppy seeds and honey or a fruit filling. Some people say the cakes are made in a triangle to remind us of the hat of Haman, the wicked enemy of the Jews. Others say it's the shape of his ear.

First guess how many hamantaschen are in the box. Then try to count them.

Answer on page 62.

CROSS OUT HAMAN

Long ago in the kingdom of Persia, Haman, a wicked minister of the king, tried to kill all the Jews. He didn't succeed. On Purim the story of the Jewish victory over Haman is read from Megillat Esther. Each time Haman's name is read we make noise to drown out his name.

HAMAN appears 30 times in the letters below. Cross out each one you find.

SAMPLE

```
H A M A N O U Y T N A M A H J O U R I M N B
H A P P Y P U R I M B V F R E W H H A W S R
N H A M A N F O U R H A M A N A T A F I V E
O N E H A M A N L O H O P U R I M S M O N E
H A M A N E S T H E R A K A R B E N H A P L
M O E D E C H A I O P U M S H A B B A T N O
H O N E H A M A N M O R E A N T H A M A N Y
B A P U R I M H A M A N O P N G E S T H E R
N B M P U Y T R E W S A C V B I N A M A H B
A B V A O H A M A N L K J H U Y T R E N B U
M U Y T N M O R D E C H A I N H G H A M A N
A E S T H E R X N A M A H W E R A M B C S A
H A M A N P A S S O V E R S O O N M B V C H
S H A V U O T N H A M A N S E V E N A W E A
M N A M A H Y O M K I P P U R M B T Y N B M
R E W S A W H A M A N H A M A N T Y R E W A
P A S S O V E R I S C O M I N G S O O N B N
H V F H A M A N E H H A P P Y P U R I M C E
A M N V F R E S A W A L O I U Y T P U R I M
M M N O U Y T E R D V M B G N A M A H A W E
A S H U S H A N W U R D A P U R I M T E R B
N S N A M A H S E V E N B N J O T H A M A N
```

Answer on page 62.

WHAT'S IN THE BAG?

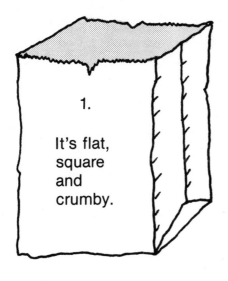

1. It's flat, square and crumby.

1. _____

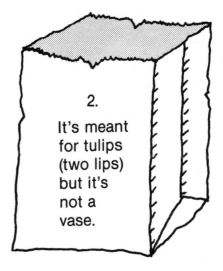

2. It's meant for tulips (two lips) but it's not a vase.

2. _____

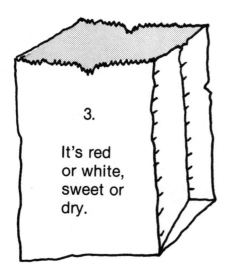

3. It's red or white, sweet or dry.

3. _____

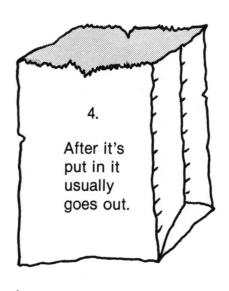

4. After it's put in it usually goes out.

4. _____

THE CHAMETZ SEARCH

Chametz is leaven, dough which has been allowed to rise. Bread is the most obvious form of chametz, but chametz is also found in cake, cookies and other things. Before Passover we search and remove all chametz from our homes. Search in the house below to find all the hidden chametz.

The word "chametz" is hidden vertically and horizontally, forwards and backwards. Each time you find one, circle it until you have found all 25. To get you started, two have already been circled.

```
              O H              C V H
              T M N I          H O T
              M A T Z O H      A R Z
              W C H A M E T Z  M K T
              H O U S E F O U R S E G E
          A C H A M E T Z S O N T B M
            C O B Z C H A M E T Z G Z L A
            W E R E T P A S S O V E R D W H
          O N E Z T E M A H C M O S E S D C V
        C T H R E E M B O Y C H A M E T Z R C S
      C H A M E T Z N O A M W C H C J W T H H R L
      B A F O U R C H A M E T Z H G H N J U A U C
      N M T R E W D C V G B C H A M E T Z U M O H
      A E C H A M E T Z O C H A M E T Z K L E W A
      A T S H O E N G G C H A M E T Z Q W R T C M
      Q Z T E M A H C T R E D S T O T W A S Z H E
      W Z T H R E E C H A M E T Z O E F O U R A T
      A T K N B V T E S        F R M        F M Z
      C E C H A M E T Z        R F A        G E V
      N M P N M O C Y R        D E H        Y T R
      A A Z T E M A H C        D S C S O N S Z W
      C H A M E T Z Y T        L P A S S O V E R
      A C P E S A C H M        C H A M E T Z E W
```

Answer on page 63.

MATZAH PICTURE RIDDLES

Below are drawings of four things made of matzah.
Can you tell what they are?

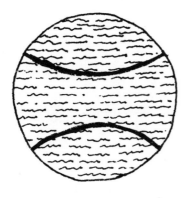

1. _____

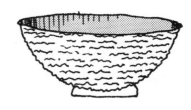

2. _____

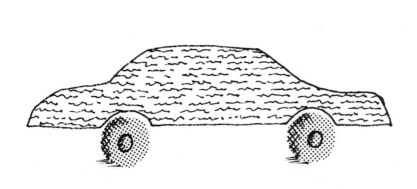

3. _____

4. _____

Answers on page 63

HOLIDAY BRAIN TEASERS

1. What is the weight of a box of matzah if it weighs 8 ounces plus half its weight?

2. If you have a large jug of Passover wine and three pitchers holding 3 cups, 5 cups, and 8 cups, how would you get exactly 4 cups in one of the pitchers?

3. If one child can eat one latke in one minute, how long would it take thirty children to eat thirty latkes?

Answers on page 63.

TO JERUSALEM FOR THE HOLIDAYS

During the years that the Temple was standing in Jerusalem, Jews traveled there to celebrate the holidays of Sukkot, Passover, and Shavuot. See if you can find your way to Jerusalem through the maze below.

JERUSALEM

Answer on page 63.

HOW MANY BOXES OF MATZAH?

Each stack of boxes is solid. Don't just count the boxes you see. Some boxes are hidden from view.

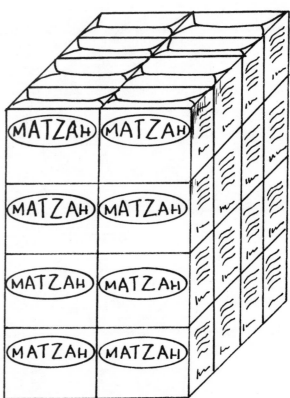

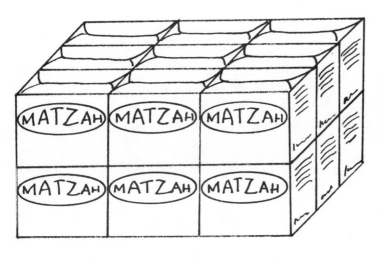

Answers on page 63.

HOLIDAY KNOCK KNOCKS

"Knock knock."
"Who's there?"
"Lulav."
"Lulav who?"
"You'll love these knock knock jokes."

"Knock knock."
"Who's there?"
"Asher."
"Asher who?"
"I sure hope this is Purim
and that's a mask you're wearing."

"Knock knock."
"Who's there?"
"Fanny."
"Fanny who?"
"If anybody wants me, I'll be in the sukkah."

"Knock knock."
"Who's there?"
"Satellites."
"Satellites who?
*"Saw the lights in the window.
Is it Chanukah already?"*

"Knock knock."
"Who's there?"
"Gwen."
"Gwen who?"
"Go in the sukkah and eat your dinner."

"Knock knock."
"Who's there?"
"Shofar."
"Shofar who?"
"So far they are not very funny."

THE BROKEN MATZAH

Which is the missing piece in this broken matzah?

Answer on page 63.

SILLY ANSWERS TO RIDICULOUS QUESTIONS

My dog wants to eat matzah on Passover. How should I make it?

Use collie flour.

What should you do if you can't be in synagogue on Rosh Hashanah to hear the shofar blown?

Get a private tooter.

Do grapes make wine?

No. You have to squeeze it out of them.

Can you tell me how long challah should be baked?

Long challah should be baked the same as short challah.

Can I take a car when I go to synagogue on Purim?

You can, but with the megillah and noisemakers you might have too much to carry. Maybe you should let the car take you.

Can you tell me what to do with the Havdallah candle after Havdallah?

Sure. I'll give you a blow-by-blow description.

Why is the afikomen always found in the last place you look?

Because when you find it, you stop looking.

HOW MANY FLAGS?

On Yom Ha'Azmaut, Israel's Independence Day, many people fly Israel's flag. It's blue and white.
How many flags are there in the box below?

Answer on page 63.

PICK SOME FLOWERS

On Shavuot we celebrate the day the Torah was given on Mount Sinai. We decorate our homes and synagogues with greens and flowers to remind us of Mount Sinai. At the time the Torah was given, the mountain was covered with greens and flowers, too.

Search through the letters below. Circle every DAFFODIL, DAISY, IRIS, ASTER, LILAC, ZINNIA, and LILY you find. There are six of each hidden in the letters below.

```
T U L I P M D A I R I S Q D A F F O D I L C V N
T O R A H R A T H E L I L A C B I R I S O N E I
I R I S V T F D A I S Y Y U I Z I N N I A G H R
S E V E N S F S H A V U O T N Y R L I L Y N M I
W E I R I S O Z I N N I A M I C H A E L T P N S
K A R B E N D H A P P Y H O L I D A Y T O Y O U
T N B G F E I C L I L Y F O U R T U L I P C V Z
U L I L A C L C X E W D A F F O D I L C T R E I
L M N I U Y T R E W A S D Z I N N I A C X E R N
I A S T E R C F R E D A I S Y M O I Y U T E C N
P C R E I O P L I T U L I P C R A S T E R B Y I
L I L A C Z E R W O L H A P P Y H O L I D A Y A
D A F F O D I L C A I G H I D A F F O D I L V B
Z E L I L Y C R T S L C Z R E W R A S T E R B K
D A D A I S Y V R T A V I L I L Y V F D R E A W
A O P I Y U G H K E C B N C U O K L I L A C C E
I B A S T E R N M R O U N C R E F T V B H G D S
S L I L A C T E R W A S I B I O P U F O U R A H
Y X E R W A Z I N N I A A B U T R L I R I S I B
C D A I S Y N M O L I L Y C E R W I X E W R S O
A S T E R F T R E W O P K L U T Y P I L I L Y X
D E T U L I P X E R Y T D A F F O D I L G H T Y
```

Answer on page 63.

HOLIDAY CROSSWORD PUZZLE #2

ACROSS

1. The seventh day of every week.
4. A book of the Bible.
6. Not off.
7. Not out.
8. Rosh Hashanah.
10. _____ B'Omer.
11. Holiday bread.
13. What adults don't do on Yom Kippur.
15. The holiday celebrating receiving the Torah.
18. Opposite of "yes."
20. Not off.
21. At what time.
22. Kiddush drink.
23. Not dry.
25. _____ Kippur.

DOWN

1. Mount _____.
2. Before Bar Mitzvah you are a _____.
3. Simchat _____.
5. Not small.
9. Havdallah drink.
10. Palm branch.
12. Not cold.
14. Dipped in honey.
15. Cold, wet and white.
16. Apples and _____.
17. Days of the _____.
19. Chanukah fuel.
24. You must go _____ school.

Answer on page 63.

HOLIDAY RIDDLES

Which burn longer, Chanukah candles or Shabbat candles?

Neither. Candles burn shorter.

How does chicken soup smell?

Fowl.

Why is the Omer depressed?

Its days are numbered.

A chicken walked into the sukkah. Where did it come from?

An egg.

What did one Shabbat candle say to the other?

"Are you going out tonight?"

How was kugel invented?

Some smart cook used his noodle.

ANSWERS

A SHABBAT MAZE

HOLIDAY SEARCH

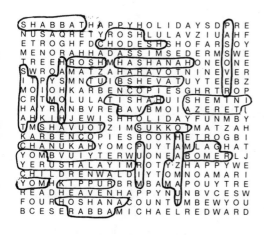

HOLIDAY REBUS

1. Simchat Torah. 2. Sukkot.
3. Tu B'Shevat. 4. Chanukah.

A SCRAMBLED SHABBAT

1. Challah. 2. Candles.
3. Wine. 4. Kiddush.

CANDLESTICK PUZZLE

Number 4.

HOLIDAY PICTURE RIDDLES

1. Fast days.
2. Candles (canned dills).
3. Passover matzah ("pass" over matzah).
4. Pesach (Pesach is the Hebrew word for Passover. That's the Hebrew letter *peh* inside a sack.)
5. A bitter Herb. (We eat bitter herbs on Passover to remember the bitter taste of slavery.)

AN APPLE AND HONEY MAZE

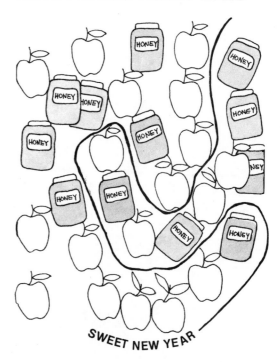

SWEET NEW YEAR

THE MISSING PIECE

Number 2.

A SCRAMBLED NEW YEAR

1. Honey. 2. Prayer.
3. Charity. 4. Shofar.

SUKKOT MAZE

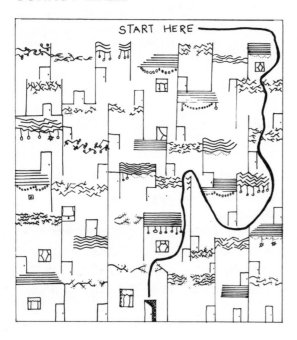

THE SUKKAH CHAIN

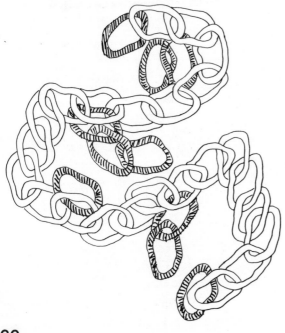

HIDDEN HOLIDAY MESSAGES

1. The Shabbat candle told the match "You burn me up."
2. Matzah is crummy.
3. Fast days are slow days.
4. I give my lulav the shakes.
5. Shabbat is never more than six days away.

LULAV, ETROG, ARAVOT, HADASSIM

There are seven full sets.

SHEMINI AZERET

A, aim, am, ant, are, arm, art, as, ash, ate, ear, eat, hair, harm, harsh, hat, hate, haze, he, hear, heart, heat, hem, hen, her, hi, him, hint, I, in, mart, mash, maze, me, mean, meant, meat, meet, men, mine, mint, mist, name, near, neat, nest, net, rain, rate, rear, rent, rim, same, sat, sea, seat, see, set, shame, she, sheet, shin, shine, shirt, sit, size, tame, tar, tea, team, tear, the, their, then, there, these, thin, this, time, tin, tire.

SIMCHAT TORAH REBUS

On Simchat Torah, the day the reading of the Five Books of Moses was completed and begun again, there was great joy. Rabbis who studied the Torah all year were singing and dancing and so were their students. But the one who was celebrating the most was a poor tailor.

"Why are you so happy?" someone asked the tailor. "You did not study the Torah all year. You did not even listen when it was being read on Shabbat and holidays."

"I don't study the Torah because I can't," the tailor answered. "I can't read Hebrew and I don't understand it. But I can dance and sing as well as anyone, so that is what I do."

CHANUKAH PUZZLES

Who lost the game of dreidel? Jane's father. *One dollar is missing:* The shopkeeper has $55 and the brothers have $3. That makes $58. Add to that the $2 the brothers gave the clerk and you have $60. *Boxed:* Put 1 candle into the first box, 1 candle into the second box, 3 candles into the third box and 2 candles into the fourth box. Then put the first box into the fourth box.

CANDLE PUZZLES

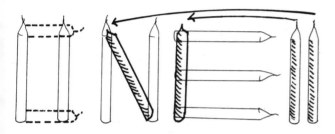

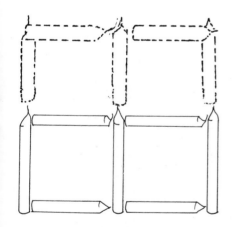

There are four small squares and one large one.

DREIDEL   MAZE

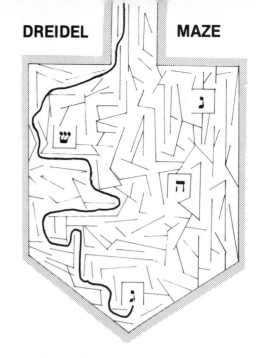

HOLIDAY CROSSWORD PUZZLE

¹C	²A	³N	⁴D	L	E	S				⁵L
U	⁶O	R	E				⁷T	⁸W	O	
⁹P	¹⁰U	R	I	M		¹¹T	R	E	E	S
	N		¹²N	O		I		N		T
	D		¹³K	N	O	W	S			
	E				N		¹⁵H	¹⁶A	M	A	¹⁷N
¹⁸O	R	¹⁹A	N	G	E		²⁰A	V		I
		P								S
²¹E	T	R	O	G			²²O			A
		I				²³S	I	V	A	N
		²⁴L	U	L	A	V		L		

DANGLED WICKS

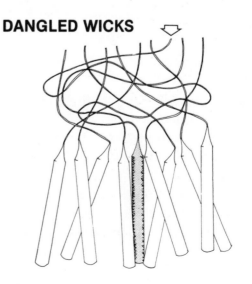

SCRAMBLED HOLIDAYS

Shavuot, Shabbat, Rosh Chodesh.

A TU B'SHEVAT MAZE

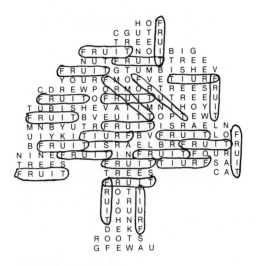

PICK SOME FRUIT

PURIM REBUS

Ahasuerus was king of the Persian Empire. He gave a seven day feast. Vashti, the queen, gave a feast for the women. On the seventh day Ahasuerus called for Vashti to come before him. He would show everyone how beautiful she was. Vashti refused to come and was sent away.

The king's men searched for someone to replace Vashti. They found a Jewish woman, Esther. She became the new queen.

Esther's cousin Mordecai lived in the capital city of Shushan. He refused to bow to the king's chief minister, Haman. Haman then planned to kill all the Jews. Ahasuerus told him he could.

Mordecai told Esther what was about to happen to her people. She spoke to the king and the Jews were saved.

HAMAN CAME IN

1. Hamantasch nosh.
2. Lotsa matzah.
3. Dreidel ladle.
4. Esther tester.
5. Torah hora.
6. Candle handle.
7. Manila Megillah.

HOW MANY HAMANTASCHEN?

Sixty.

CROSS OUT HAMAN

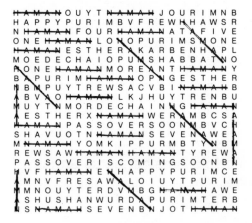

THE CHAMETZ SEARCH

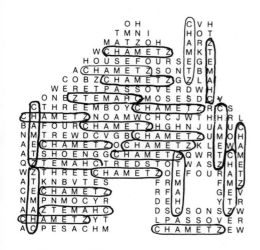

MATZAH PICTURE RIDDLES

1. A matzah ball. 2. A matzah bowl.
3. A matzahmobile.
4. A matzah magician.

HOLIDAY BRAIN TEASERS

1. Sixteen ounces.
2. Fill the 5 cup pitcher with wine.
Pour from the 5 cup pitcher into the 3
cup pitcher until the 3 cup pitcher is
full. Exactly two cups will remain in
the 5 cup pitcher. Pour the two cups
into the 8 cup pitcher. Do this all
again and exactly four cups will be in
the 8 cup pitcher. 3. One minute.

TO JERUSALEM FOR THE HOLIDAYS

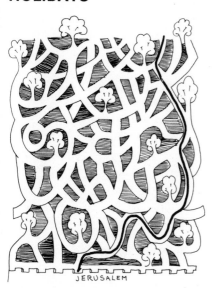

HOW MANY BOXES OF MATZAH?

4, 18, 32.

THE BROKEN MATZAH

4.

HOW MANY FLAGS?

30.

PICK SOME FLOWERS

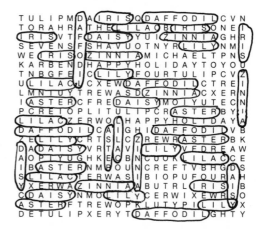

HOLIDAY CROSSWORD PUZZLE #2